MILKWEED FOR MONARCHS

by **Christine Van Zandt**
illustrated by **Alejandra Barajas**

beaming ☀ books
MINNEAPOLIS

Flitter, flutter,
wings flash in the sun.
The weather has warmed.
Migration's begun.

North, forth,
they fly on the breeze . . .

. . . beyond human borders,
then shelter in trees.

Each year there are four generations of monarchs.

The longer-living fourth generation migrates south
when temperatures cool.

When overwintering is complete, butterflies return north.

Bare, there,
it's harder each year
to find the right plants
when fields are now clear.

Perching, searching,
scanning the ground,
a hunt never ending . . .

. . . 'til milkweed is found.

Monarchs need milkweed; it's the only plant their caterpillars can eat.

Potted, spotted!
Mother glides through the air.

She lands like a breath . . .
and lays eggs with care.

STAGE 1:

EGG (3–5 DAYS)

A monarch butterfly returns to lay eggs on the milkweed where her ancestors hatched.

Deciding where she lays each egg strongly affects the egg's ability to survive.

Laying too many eggs on one plant may mean not enough food for all of her young.

Placed, spaced,
eggs tucked out of sight.
Some nectar to sip . . .

She rises in flight.

An egg is about the size of the period at the end of a sentence.

The 300–500 eggs a butterfly lays over her short lifetime seem like a lot, but survival is hard.

An egg is easy prey for predators and is hurt by some of the chemicals people use on plants.

Tiny, shiny,
in the sun's beams.
While deep down inside . . .

A new monarch dreams.

An egg's waxy covering keeps it from drying out.

The amount of sunshine and the temperature
are factors in how soon an egg hatches.

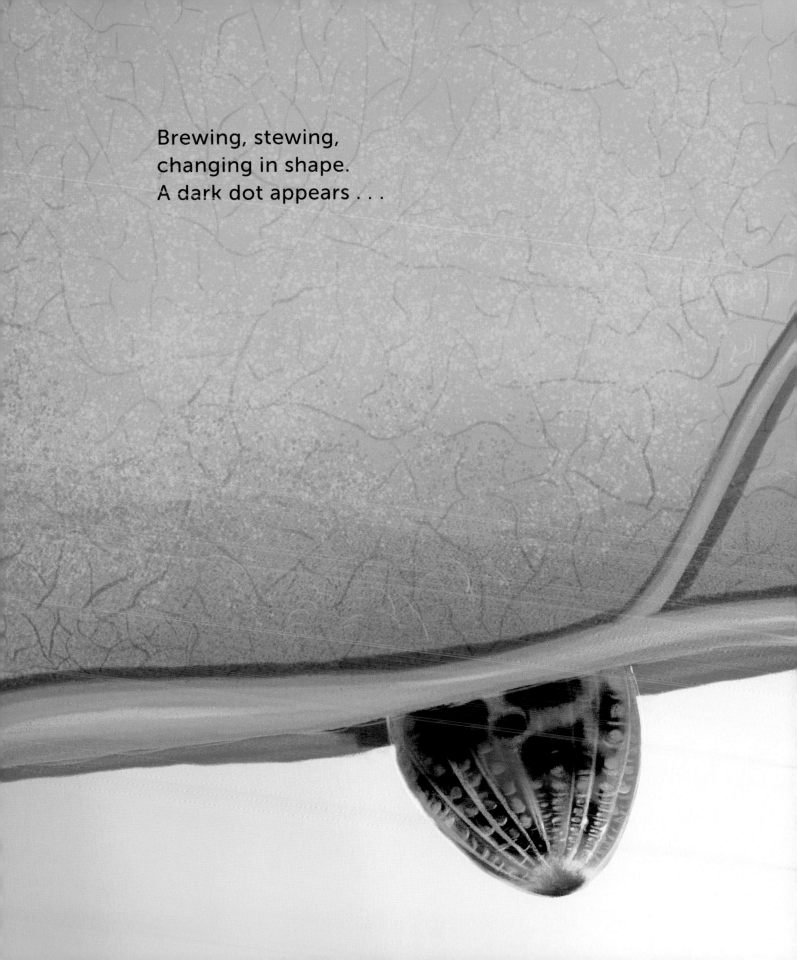

Brewing, stewing,
changing in shape.
A dark dot appears . . .

Then the escape!

STAGE 2:

CATERPILLAR, ALSO CALLED LARVA (11–18 DAYS)

The spot at the top of the egg is the caterpillar's head.

The caterpillar chews its way out, then eats the eggshell.

Though monarchs are herbivores, caterpillars sometimes eat other eggs.

Life, strife,
the odds are not high.
But *this* little one
is eager to try.

Chew through
that milkweed leaf.
Better be quick or . . .

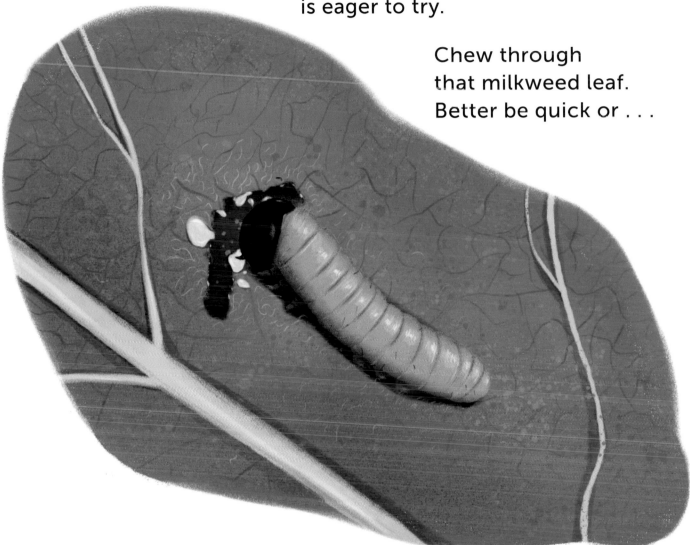

Milkweed defends itself with leaf hairs
that a caterpillar must eat through before
reaching the leaf itself.

When a caterpillar bites into a leaf, latex gushes
out—it's like trying to drink from a fire hydrant.

The caterpillar is smaller than a grain of rice,
and its pale color provides camouflage.

Time here is brief.

A caterpillar may be caught in a spider's web
or carried off by an ant.

By laying a line of silk, a caterpillar can quickly
drop and dangle, dodging danger.

Strange change,
what happened to green?

Now "Stay away!" stripes are easily seen.

A caterpillar's yellow, black, and white stripes warn predators to stay away.

Eating milkweed protects monarchs because they retain a bit of the plant's toxins.

When a bird eats a monarch caterpillar, it may feel sick and learn not to eat one again.

Crunching, munching,
then it excretes.
A growth spurt, some rest . . .

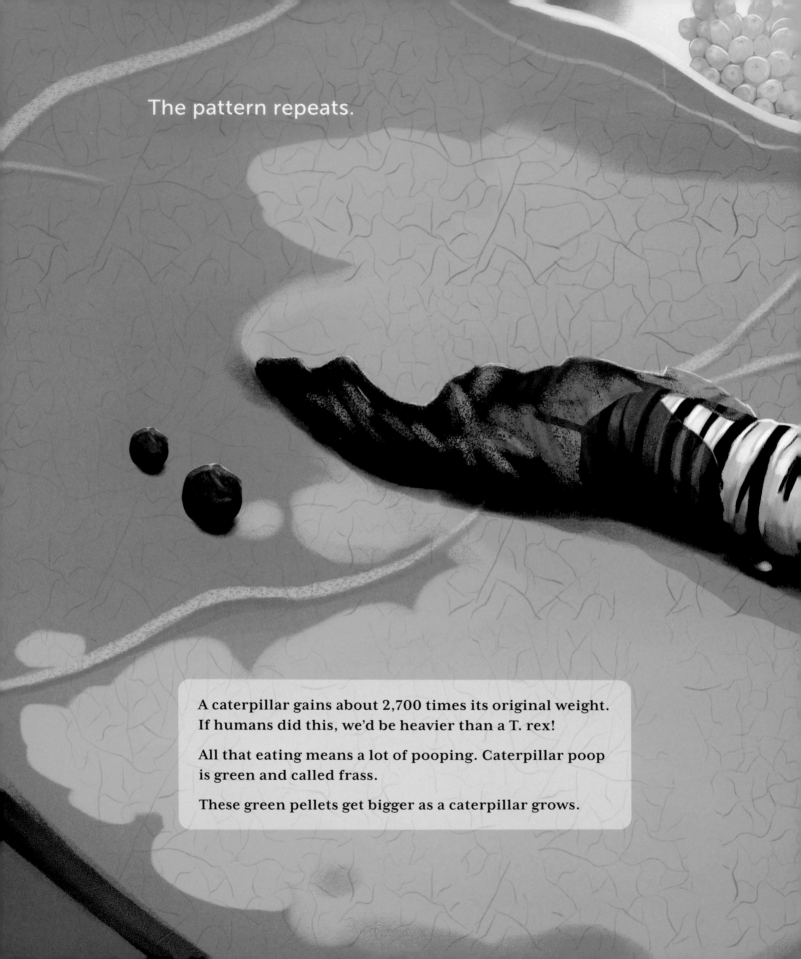

The pattern repeats.

A caterpillar gains about 2,700 times its original weight. If humans did this, we'd be heavier than a T. rex!

All that eating means a lot of pooping. Caterpillar poop is green and called frass.

These green pellets get bigger as a caterpillar grows.

Slooow so
skin can be shed . . .

. . . 'til the right place is found
to spin silky thread.

When a caterpillar becomes too large for
its skin, it molts (sheds its skin).

The stages of an insect's life between molts
are called instars.

Caterpillars molt five times as they grow.
The final molt reveals the chrysalis (pupa).

Wiggling, jiggling,
while shaped like a J,
the pupa's revealed . . .

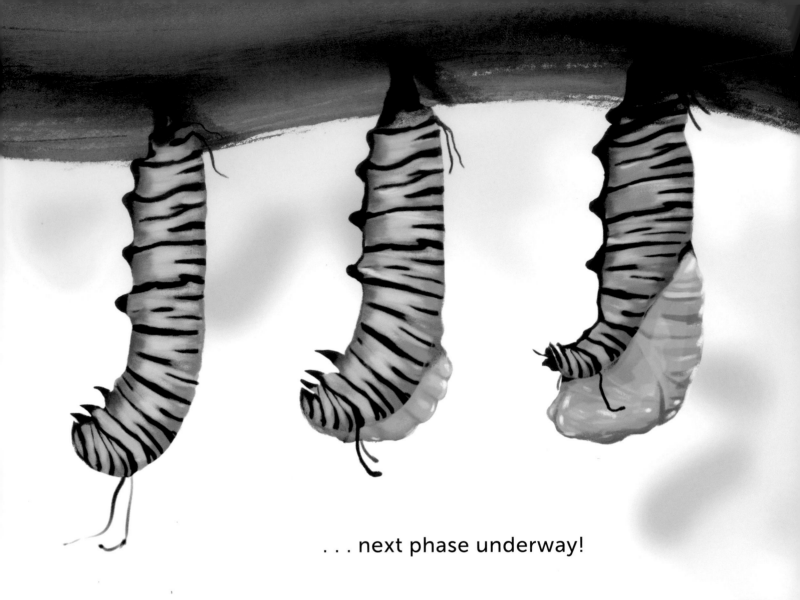

. . . next phase underway!

STAGE 3:

CHRYSALIS, ALSO CALLED PUPA (8–14 DAYS); METAMORPHOSIS BEGINS

A caterpillar spins a white silk mat in a safe spot to secure itself before molting into a chrysalis.

It hangs head down in a J-shape. Starting from the head, the skin pushes up and off.

After a few hours, the outside of the chrysalis (exoskeleton) hardens to protect the soft insides.

Bold, gold,
the chrysalis gleams.
And deep down inside . . .

The butterfly dreams.

A chrysalis's leaf-green color and reflective, metallic-like gold accents provide camouflage.

The gold color is created by the milkweed's pigments (carotenoids) and the chrysalis's ridges.

While the chrysalis seems green, it's actually the green pupa inside that we see.

Inside, the body parts of a caterpillar are changing to those of a butterfly.

Stays, days,
transforming within.
When colors surprise . . .

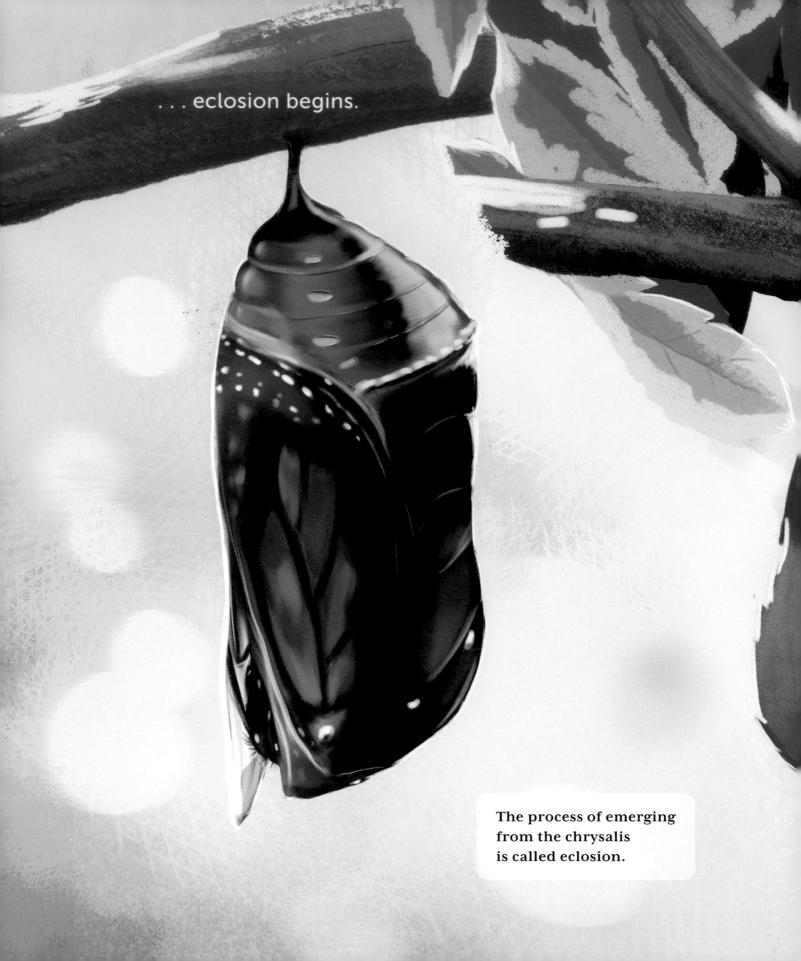

. . . eclosion begins.

The process of emerging
from the chrysalis
is called eclosion.

Things? Wings!
Orange and black.
Pushing out of the shell . . .

legs emerge
from a crack.

STAGE 4:

BUTTERFLY

First, the legs appear, then the rest of the butterfly slides out.

Wrinkled, crinkled.
The wet wings must dry.
In a few hours . . .

Holding onto its empty exoskeleton or a nearby branch, unable to fly for hours, the butterfly is vulnerable.

This monarch will fly!

Once the wings begin to flap, you can tell whether it's a male or a female.

A male butterfly has two black spots on its hind wings. A female butterfly does not.

Flitter, flutter,
too soon it seems,
our mother gives birth . . .

. . . to new monarch dreams.

AUTHOR'S NOTE

In 2020, during the at-home time brought on by the pandemic, my daughter and I noticed our yard's little things—*very* little things, such as monarch butterfly eggs on our milkweed plants. We watched the caterpillars grow and learned that monarch butterflies travel from flower to flower, pollinating plants, enabling them to develop fruit and seeds. Monarchs are also an important part of the food web because they are prey for other insects, spiders, birds, lizards, and mammals.

However, food sources for monarchs are disappearing; if they become extinct, other animals and plants will be affected. But this doesn't have to happen. Home gardeners and schools can grow native milkweed and flowers. Munched milkweed leaves mean monarchs in the making!

What we know about the world is always changing. Become a citizen scientist and seek out the latest information. By being curious, we can work together to help the monarchs.

MONARCHS NEED OUR HELP

The population of western monarchs has declined by 95 percent over the last forty years. Previously, 4.5 million overwintered along the West Coast; in November 2020, only 1,914 monarchs were counted. Eastern monarch populations overwintering primarily in Mexico's mountains are following patterns of decline as well.

Humans pose the most serious threat. Dangers include pesticides, herbicides, and pollen from corn whose genes have been altered to kill "pests." Monarch habitats are decreasing because milkweed is being removed so the land can be used for farming, logging, and housing. Also, pollution is harmful to monarchs, as it is to us.

Monarchs are bioindicators, sensitive to what's happening in the world. A drop in their number may indicate bigger problems in an ecosystem, such as the widespread effects from climate change's global warming.

Even though the 2021 monarch count showed an increase in the population, monarchs are far from safe. In July 2022, the International Union for Conservation of Nature (IUCN) reclassified migratory monarchs as "endangered."

HOW YOU CAN HELP

1. Grow milkweed for monarch caterpillars and flowers for butterflies—other insects and birds will benefit too!

2. Don't use harmful chemicals in your garden.

3. Start a school or community garden.

4. Spread the word: Because plants make oxygen and reduce greenhouse gases, they help people and the planet.

FUN FACTS

Q. How many legs do monarch caterpillars have?
A. Six, but it seems like they have many more because they also have five pairs of false legs.

Q. How many legs do monarch butterflies have?
A. Six, but they only use four legs, keeping the first pair tucked away.

Q. Why can we hear a mosquito's wings but not a butterfly's wings?
A. Even though butterflies are bigger than mosquitoes, their wings beat more slowly.

Q. What do monarch butterflies have in common with bees?
A. Monarch butterflies are also pollinators.

Q. How much does a monarch butterfly weigh?
A. It weighs about half a gram or as much as half of a dollar bill.

THE SENSES
(SOUND, SMELL, TASTE, TOUCH, AND SIGHT)

A monarch butterfly's ears are at the base of its wings, about the same place where humans have armpits.

Monarch butterflies smell with their antennae, which are densely covered with chemoreceptors. These are also located on their legs to help females find milkweed.

Caterpillars can only eat, and butterflies can only drink. Butterflies taste with their feet. They drink through a straw-like tongue called a proboscis that uncurls to sip nectar and water.

Caterpillars and butterflies sense touch through fine hairs called setae.

A butterfly's relatively enormous compound eyes are made up of thousands of small simple eyes, each of which senses light and images. They can see up, down, forward, backward, and to the sides at the same time.

Selected Bibliography

Agrawal, Anurag. *Monarchs and Milkweed: A Migrating Butterfly, a Poisonous Plant, and Their Remarkable Story of Coevolution.* Princeton: Princeton University Press, 2017.

Bové, Jennifer. *Ranger Rick: I Wish I Was a Monarch Butterfly.* New York: HarperCollins, 2019.

Hammer, Joshua. "An Epic Monarch Migration Faces New Threats." *Smithsonian*, May 20, 2021, https://www.smithsonianmag.com/science-nature/epic-monarch-butterfly-migration-faces-threats-180977449/.

McCarthy, Cecilia Pinto. *Monarch Butterflies Matter (Bioindicator Species).* Minneapolis: Abdo Publishing, 2016.

Rice, Doyle. "Monarch Butterflies Won't Get Legal Protection, Despite Meeting 'Endangered' Criteria." *USA Today*, December 16, 2020, https://www.usatoday.com/story/news/nation/2020/12/15/monarch-butterflies-endangered-legal-protection/3905631001/.

To the monarch caterpillar named Houdini
who started me on this amazing journey—CVZ

To my dear family for supporting me at all times—AB

Text copyright © 2024 Christine Van Zandt
Illustrations by Alejandra Barajas, copyright © 2024 Beaming Books

29 28 27 26 25 24 23   1 2 3 4 5 6 7 8

Hardcover ISBN: 978-1-5064-8930-8
eBook ISBN: 978-1-5064-8931-5

Library of Congress Cataloging-in-Publication Data
Names: Van Zandt, Christine, author. | Barajas, Alejandra, illustrator.
Title: Milkweed for monarchs / by Christine Van Zandt ; illustrated by
    Alejandra Barajas.
Description: Minneapolis, MN : Beaming Books, 2024. | Includes
    bibliographical references. | Audience: Ages 4-8 | Summary: "This
    lyrical picture book looks at the lifecycle of the monarch butterfly and
    conveys the need to care for our planet"-- Provided by publisher.
Identifiers: LCCN 2023004992 (print) | LCCN 2023004993 (ebook) | ISBN
    9781506489308 (Hardcover) | ISBN 9781506489315 (eBook)
Subjects: LCSH: Monarch butterfly--Life cycles--Juvenile literature. |
    Milkweeds--Juvenile literature. | Monarch butterfly--Life
    cycles--Juvenile poetry.
Classification: LCC QL561.N9 V36 2024 (print) | LCC QL561.N9 (ebook) |
    DDC 595.78/9--dc23/eng/20230424
LC record available at https://lccn.loc.gov/2023004992
LC ebook record available at https://lccn.loc.gov/2023004993

Beaming Books
PO Box 1209
Minneapolis, MN 55440-1209
Beamingbooks.com

Printed in China.